What's in this book

学习内容 Contents   2

读一读 Read   4

听听说说 Listen and say   12

写一写 Write   16

多元学习 Connections   18

温习 Checkpoint   20

分享 Sharing   22

This book belongs to

_____

你叫什么名字?
What is your name?

学习内容 Contents

沟通 Communication

介绍自己和他人
Introduce yourself and others

询问他人的名字
Ask for someone's name

生词 New words

★	你	you
★	我	I, me
★	叫	to call, to be called
★	什么	what
★	名字	name
	他	he, him
	她	she, her
	谢谢	thanks

School bus

你叫什么名字？　　　What is your name?

我叫艾文。　　　　　My name is Ivan. (I am called Ivan.)

他叫什么名字？　　　What is his name?

他叫依森。　　　　　His name is Ethan. (He is called Ethan.)

文化 Cultures

姓名的排列方式
Order of names

跨学科学习 Project

制作图章，介绍自己
Make a name stamp and
introduce yourself

Get ready

1 Where are the children?

2 Where are they going?

3 Can you find the pair of twins?

你好！你叫什么名字？

我叫艾文，他叫伊森。

伊森，这是你的玩具熊。

浩浩，谢谢！

你叫什么名字?

我叫伊森，他叫艾文。

Let's think

Number the pictures. Act out the story.

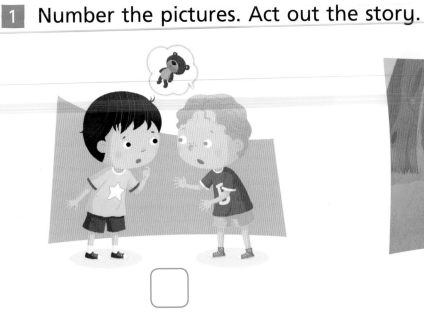

2 Circle the differences between the twins and say their names.

New words

1 Learn the new words.

2 Match the words to the pictures. Write the letters.

a 你　　b 我　　c 名字　　d 什么

1 ☐　　2 ☐　　3 ☐　　4 ☐

🎧 03 **1** Look, listen and repeat.

🎧 04 **2** Look at the pictures. Listen to the sto

...nd say.

你好，我叫布朗尼。

他叫超人。

3 Tick and say the correct sentence.

☐ 什么名字你叫？
☐ 你叫什么名字？

4 Talk with your friend.

你叫什么名字？

我叫……

Task

Find out the names of your friends.
Write them on the name tags.

你叫什么
名字？

Game

Listen to your teacher. Point to the words
and work out the sentences.

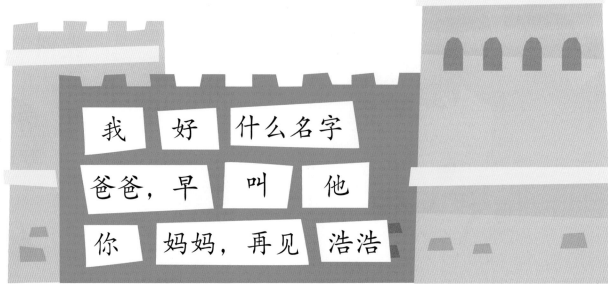

我　好　什么名字

爸爸，早　叫　他

你　妈妈，再见　浩浩

Song

Listen and sing.

你好！你好！

你好吗？

你叫什么名字？

我很好呀，我很好！

我叫浩浩！

你叫什么名字？

我叫浩浩。

课堂用语 Classroom language

很好。
Very good.

对。
Correct.

不对。
Incorrect.

对不对？
Is it correct?

1 Learn and trace the stroke.

撇

2 Learn the component. Trace 亻 to complete the characters.

你 他 们 伊

3 How many 亻 can you find in the picture? Circle them.

4 Trace and write the character.

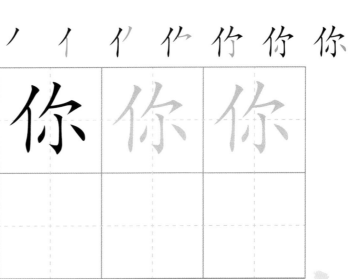

5 Write and say.

叫什么名字？

汉字 小常识 *Did you know?*

Colour the left component red and the right component green.

Some characters are made up of left and right components.

你 好 叫 什 他

多元学习 Connections

Cultures

1 What is the difference between Chinese and Western names?

Chinese names start with the family name.

王　小　玲　丁　浩

Elsa　Lopez

Western names usually end with the family name.

Peter　George　Dixon

2 Colour the family names red and the first names blue.

丁　玲　Ethan　Joseph　Jones

Project

1 Make yourself a name stamp.

Be careful!

2 Stamp your name below and say it.

我叫 Alice。你叫什么名字？

温习 Checkpoint

1 Ethan lost his teddy bear. Help him find it.

Finish

Write 'you' in Chinese.

2 Work with your friend. Colour the stars and the chillies.

Words and sentences	说	读	写
你	☆	☆	☆
我	☆	☆	🌶
叫	☆	☆	🌶
什么	☆	☆	🌶
名字	☆	☆	🌶
他	☆	🌶	🌶
她	☆	🌶	🌶
谢谢	☆	🌶	🌶
你叫什么名字？	☆	🌶	🌶
我叫浩浩。	☆	🌶	🌶

Introduce yourself and others	☆
Ask for someone's name	☆

3 What does your teacher say?

My teacher says ...

分享 Sharing

Words I remember

你	nǐ	you
我	wǒ	I, me
叫	jiào	to call, to be called
什么	shén me	what
名字	míng zi	name
他	tā	he, him
她	tā	she, her
谢谢	xiè xie	thanks

Other words

伊森	yī sēn	Ethan
艾文	ài wén	Ivan
这	zhè	this
是	shì	to be
的	de	of
玩具熊	wán jù xióng	teddy bear

OXFORD
UNIVERSITY PRESS

Oxford University Press is a department of the University of Oxford.
It furthers the University's objective of excellence in research, scholarship,
and education by publishing worldwide. Oxford is a registered trade mark of
Oxford University Press in the UK and in certain other countries

Published in Hong Kong by
Oxford University Press (China) Limited
39th Floor, One Kowloon, 1 Wang Yuen Street, Kowloon Bay,
Hong Kong

Illustrated by Anne Lee and Wildman

Photographs for reproduction permitted by Dreamstime.com

China National Publications Import & Export (Group) Corporation is an authorized distributor of
Oxford Elementary Chinese.

Please contact content@cnpiec.com.cn or 86-10-65856782

ISBN: 978-0-19-942969-1

10 9 8 7 6 5 4 3 2

Teacher's Edition
ISBN: 978-0-19-082146-7
10 9 8 7 6 5 4 3 2